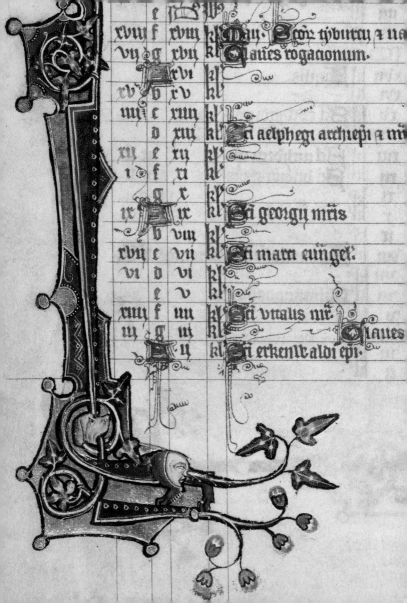

	e	[xix]	[kl]	
xviii	f	xviii	kl	May · Geor̄ tyburcii ꝗ ua...
vij	g	xvij	kl	Claues rogacionum.
	A	xvi	kl	
xv	b	xv	kl	
iiij	c	xiiij	kl	
	d	xiij	kl	Sci aelphegi archiepi ꝗ mi...
xij	e	xij	kl	
i	f	xi	kl	
	g	x	kl	
ix	A	ix	kl	Sci georgij mr̄is
	b	viij	kl	
xvij	c	vij	kl	Sci marci euu̅gel̄.
vi	d	vi	kl	
	e	v	kl	
xiiij	f	iiij	kl	Sci vitalis mr̄.
iij	g	iij	kl	Claues
	A	ij	kl	Sci erkenn̅ aldi epi·

The Macclesfield Psalter

'... a window into the world
of late medieval England'

The
Fitzwilliam
Museum

The discovery of an unsuspected treasure

The Macclesfield Psalter is the most remarkable English illuminated manuscript to be discovered in living memory. With the vast majority of frescos and panels destroyed by religious zeal, social unrest, or subsequent neglect, this tiny book (170 x 108 mm), with its supple parchment, glowing gold and precious pigments, is a rare witness to the refined beauty and ribald humour of English medieval painting. Works of art of such age and quality no longer escape the attention of scholars and art dealers, even when kept in private collections. Completely unknown,

the Macclesfield Psalter rested on the shelves at Shirburn Castle for centuries, until the Library of the Earl of Macclesfield began to be dispersed at auction in 2004.

As the leading fine art museum in the East of England and the home of an outstanding manuscript collection, the Fitzwilliam Museum tried to acquire the manuscript at the Sotheby's sale on 22 June 2004. It was purchased by the J. Paul Getty Museum, Los Angeles. The Reviewing Committee on the Export of Works of Art awarded a starred rating to the manuscript and the Arts Minister placed a temporary export bar on it, recommending that every effort should be made to keep it in a public institution in this country. The National Art

Collections Fund launched a public appeal on behalf of the Fitzwilliam Museum. In addition to the Museum's own funds and contributions from its Friends, major grants from the National Heritage Memorial Fund, the National Art Collections Fund, the Cadbury Trust, and the Friends of the National Libraries were supplemented with generous donations from a large number of Trusts and individuals. This was a campaign in which no contribution was too small. The support of the public was astounding and cannot be measured in figures. It secured the future of the manuscript in this country and in the region where it was created seven centuries ago.

The East Anglian context

The Macclesfield Psalter is a splendid example of medieval art from East Anglia, which boasted one of the most inventive schools of painting in the fourteenth century.

East Anglian manuscripts combine traditional devotional imagery with closely observed nature, and charming glimpses of every-day life with bold creations of the wildest imagination. The Macclesfield Psalter is the missing link – textual, iconographic, and stylistic – between two of the finest East Anglian manuscripts, the Gorleston Psalter of around 1320 (London, British Library, Add. MS 49622) and the Douai Psalter of the 1330s, which was almost completely destroyed during the Great War (Douai, Bibliothèque municipale, MS 171). Both are associated with the parish church of St Andrew at Gorleston, near Yarmouth. Their Calendars have the dedication of the church on 8 March written in gold, exceptional treatment reserved only for the most

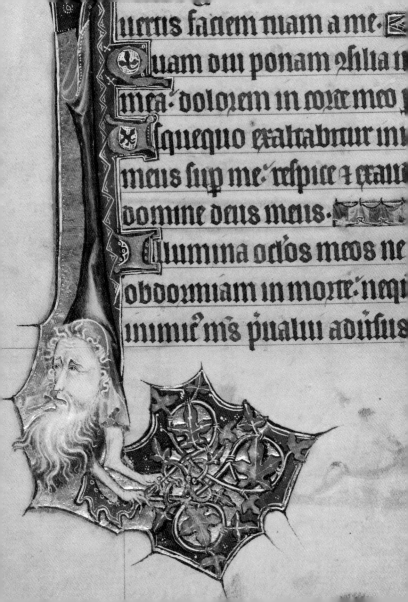

uertis faciem tuam a me ·

Quam diu ponam consilia i[n]

mea · dolorem in corde meo p[er]

squequo exaltabitur ini[micus]

meus sup me · respice + exau[di]

domine deus meus ·

Illumina oclos meos ne

obdormiam in morte · neq[ue]

inimic[us] me[us] p[re]ualui adu[er]sus

important feasts in the liturgical year, such as Christmas or Easter.

The dedication of St Andrew's church at Gorleston is absent from the Macclesfield Calendar. The manuscript opens with two full-page miniatures: St Edmund of Bury, the patron of East Anglia, is followed by St Andrew, one of the most popular saints of the Western Church. The landscape of medieval England was dotted with churches and chapels dedicated to St Andrew, including one of the richest parish churches in Norwich. The miniature of St Andrew may, of

FAR RIGHT:
St Edmund
(fol. 1r,
detail)

Joannes Smeaton,

course, reflect a patron's devotion to the saint without any association with a specific church. Indeed, St Edmund and St Andrew may have been in the company of other saints if the two leaves now missing at the beginning of the Macclesfield Psalter contained images.

Although the association with Gorleston is far from certain, the manuscript's origin and intended use in East Anglia are confirmed by its Calendar and Litany, both of Sarum use and pointing to the diocese of Norwich. St Edmund and St Etheldreda loom large. The Calendar and Litany of the Macclesfield Psalter probably served as the exemplar for those in the Douai Psalter, but derive from the liturgical apparatus of the Stowe Breviary, a manuscript made around 1325 for a religious patron in the diocese of Norwich (London, British Library, MS Stowe 12). The Calendars in the three manuscripts were written in the same peculiar combination of alternating blue,

bright and dark red inks. The Gorleston, Douai and Macclesfield Psalters, and the Stowe Breviary share an elegant Gothic bookhand with idiosyncratic letter forms and abbreviations, as well as the rather unusual choice of elaborate documentary script for the catchwords (the first words of a new gathering of leaves that were written on the last page of the previous gathering). The script of the Macclesfield Psalter is particularly close to that of the Stowe Breviary. Detailed analysis may reveal whether any of these manuscripts were copied by the same scribe, allowing for variations in scale and development of style in the course of two decades, or by several hands rigorously schooled in the same tradition.

The Stowe Breviary also preserves the earliest examples of the ornamental vocabulary specific to the Macclesfield Psalter and not present in the earlier Gorleston Psalter, notably the green and orange trilobes, the triangular leaves patterned in a white fan-like web, and the green branches with pink or purple bells. These elements, combined with the delicate pink flowers and the clusters of lush, fleshy gold leaves first found in the Macclesfield Psalter, reappear in the Douai Psalter and in two contemporary and equally elaborate volumes, the Ormesby and St Omer Psalters (Oxford, Bodleian Library, MS Douce 366 and London, British Library, Yates Thompson MS 14). These deluxe manuscripts and others, more distantly related to them, were intended for a wide range of patrons in the diocese of Norwich, from aristocratic families to their chaplains and from the vicars of parish churches to members of monastic houses. Professional scribes and artists could travel far to work on a prestigious commission, but would normally gravitate towards the focal points of commercial, ecclesiastical and intellectual activities that offered continuous

RIGHT:
Man and
bird (fol. 10v,
detail)

RIGHT:
The
Anointing
of David;
trumpeters
(fol. 39r,
detail)

OVERLEAF:
David
praying;
riding
backwards
(fols. 182v–
183r, detail)

employment on a variety of projects. The surviving East Anglian manuscripts share iconography, ornamental vocabulary, scribal, stylistic, and liturgical features which suggest a network of closely collaborating individuals, and a continuity of calligraphic and artistic traditions at a major center that could cater for a most diverse clientele. With its expanding economy, vibrant religious life, and well-documented artistic community, Norwich would have attracted both the talented and the wealthy. The international climate and intellectual vigour of Cambridge would have had a lot to offer to artists and patrons who appreciated the novelty and sophistication found in the Macclesfield Psalter. Further research may uncover more specific evidence to confirm or reject such working hypotheses.

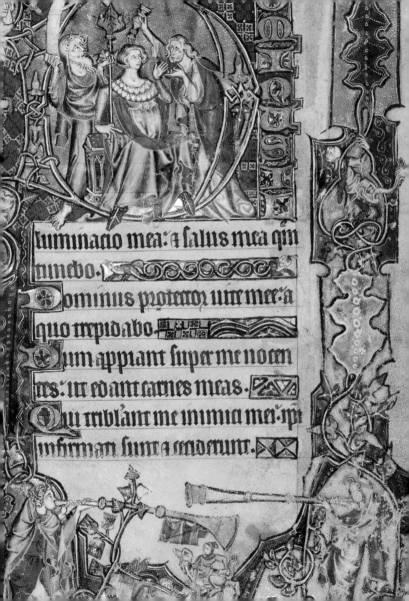

luminacio mea: a salus mea qm
nimebo.

Dominus protector uite mee· a
quo trepidabo. ꝯ

um appiant super me noceñ
tes. ut edant carnes meas·

Qui triblant me inimici mei· ipi
infirmati sunt a ceciderunt· ꝯ

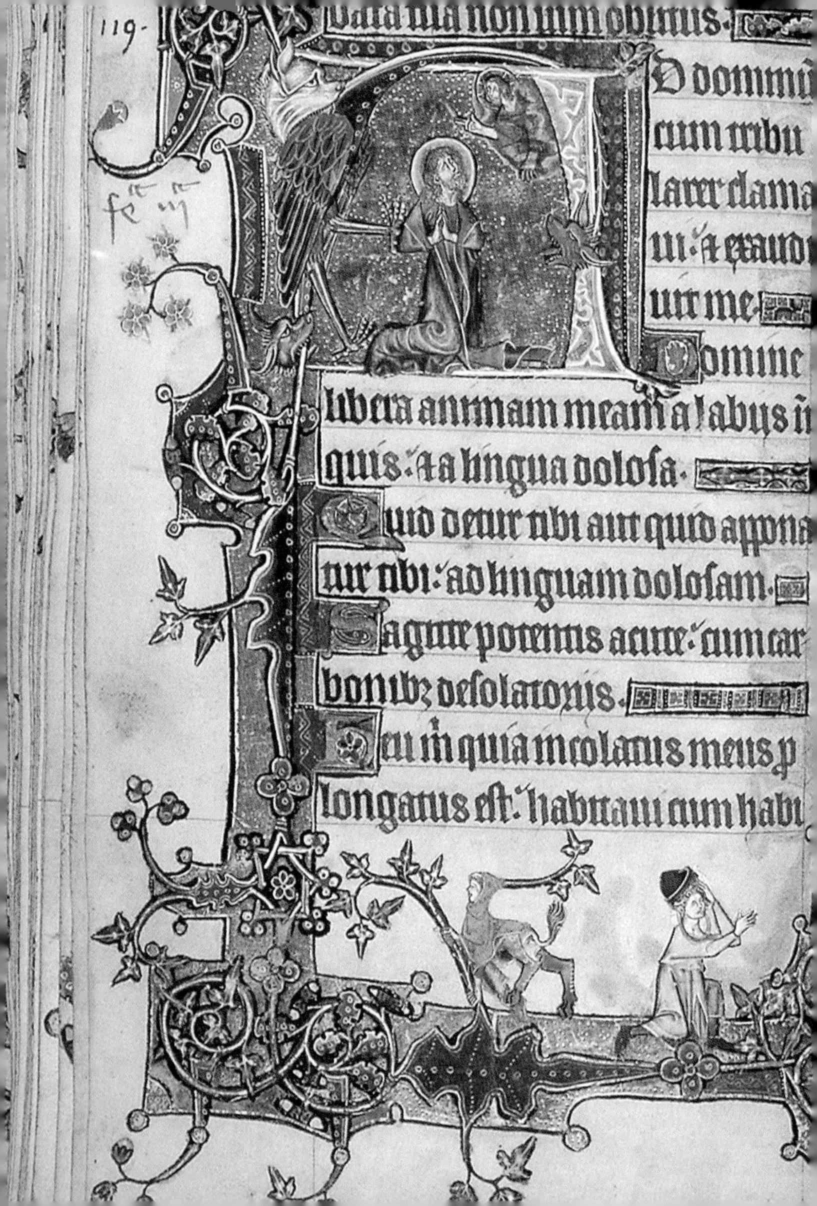

119

fe iij

bata tua non sum oblitus.

Ad dominu[m]
cum tribu
larer clama
ui . et exaudi
uit me.
Domine
libera animam meam a labiis in
quis . et a lingua dolosa.
Quid detur tibi aut quid apponat
ur tibi : ad linguam dolosam.
Sagitte potentis acute : cum car
bonibus desolatoriis.
Heu mihi quia incolatus meus p
longatus est : habitaui cum habi

anima mea.

cum hiis qui oderunt pacem eram
pacificus: cum loquebar illis impug-
nabant me gratis.

Levaui oclos meos in montes. 120.
unde ueniat auxilium michi.

Auxilium meum a domino: q
fecit celum et terram.

Non det in comocionem pedem tuu:
neque dormitet qui custodit te.

Ecce non dormitabit neque dormi-
et: qui custodit istrl.

Dominus custodit te dominus protectio tua:
super manum dexteram tuam.

Per diem sol non uret te. neque

	e	xviii	kl Assumpcio sce mar[ie]
xij	d	xvij	kl
i	e	xvi	kl Oct. sci laurency
	f	xv	kl Sci agapiti mris
ix	g	xiiij	kl Sci magni mris
	A	xiij	kl
xvij	b	xij	kl
vi	c	xi	kl Oct. sce marie.
	d	x	kl Scor tymothei z ap[?]
xiiij	e	ix	kl Sci bartholomei ap[li]
iij	f	viij	kl
	g	vij	kl
xi	A	vi	kl Sci rufi mris
xix	b	v	kl Sci augustini docto[ris]
	c	iiij	kl Decollacio sci iohis b[apt]
viij	d	iij	kl Scor felicis z adauc[ti]
	e	ij	kl Sce cuthburge virg[inis]

The text and
its illustrations

The 252 leaves of the manuscript contain the texts typical of a Gothic Psalter. The twelve pages of the Calendar list the most important feasts of Christ, the Virgin, and the saints for each month. Next comes a prayer for God's protection of the person reciting the Psalms out of this very book. The plea for his salvation is reinforced by a miniature of Christ at the Last Judgement. The volume continues with the 150 Psalms, the biblical Canticles, the Litany of saints, short prayers, the Office of the Dead, and more prayers. It concludes with the ultimate expression of penance and hope for forgiveness, the Confession prayer.

Throughout the entire medieval period, the Psalms were the central text of liturgical and devotional practices. Psalters were among the most frequently and sumptuously illuminated manuscripts. In addition to the miniatures of St Edmund, St Andrew, and Christ, the Macclesfield Psalter contains the universally established form of Gothic Psalm illustration – the historiated initials at the ten major text divisions. The letters framing elaborate scenes mark the Psalms of the three-fold division (Psalms 1, 51, and 101) and those of the so-called liturgical division. The latter includes the first Psalm in each group chanted at the midnight service from Sunday till Saturday (Psalms 1, 26, 38, 52, 68, 80, and 97) and at Sunday Vespers (Psalm 109). In addition to the ten division Psalms, the Macclesfield Psalter marked the first Gradual Psalm, 119, with an historiated initial showing David in prayer. In their private devotional exercises and prayer books, lay people emulated the routines and readings of religious communities.

RIGHT:
The Tree of
Jesse (fol. 9r,
detail)

The historiated initials to the ten division Psalms in the Macclesfield Psalter combine various approaches to the text. The Tree of Jesse sums up the genealogy of Christ and the story of human salvation at the beginning of Psalm 1, which encapsulates the meaning of the entire Psalter, the symbolic relationship between the Old and New Testaments, between David and Christ.

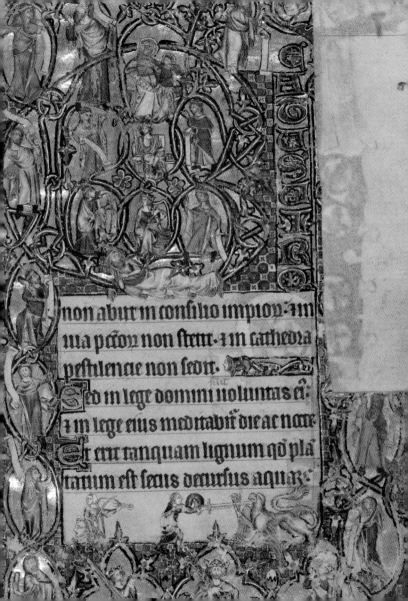

non abiit in consilio impiov̄ · in
uia p̄ccov̄ non stetit · et in cathedra
pestilencie non sedit.

Sed in lege domini uoluntas ei̯
et in lege eius meditabit̄ die ac nocte

Et erit tanquam lignum q̄d pla
tatum est secus decursus aquav̄

The initial to Psalm 26 reflects the historical context in which it was composed – the Anointing of David. Biblical narrative marks the next two major text divisions, Psalms 38 and 51, but the events depicted within the initials also serve as examples of the arrogant speech and brutal force denounced in the Psalm text. At Psalm 38 King Saul despatches Doec the Edomite to kill the priests of Nob. Doec carries out the king's order at Psalm 51. The angel announces Christ's birth to the shepherds at the beginning of Psalm 97, whose opening verses were interpreted as a prophecy of the Incarnation and sung at the feast of the Nativity. The Father and the Son share an elaborate throne at the beginning of Psalm 109, 'The Lord said to my Lord: you shall sit at my right hand'. The initials for Psalms 68, 80, and 101 are now

RIGHT:
Saul sending
Doeg to kill
the priests
of Nob; a
horseman,
a lady, and
a wildman
(fol. 58r,
detail)

detrahebant michi: qm sequebar
bonitatem.

Ne derelinquas me domine ds
meus: ne discesseris a me.

Intende in adiutorium meu:
domine deus salutis mee.

io glorī
in malicia.
qui potens
es in iniquitate.
tota die i
ustitiam co

gitauit lingua tua: sicut nouacu
la acuta fecisti dolum.

Dilexisti maliciam super benig
nitatem: iniquitatem magis q̄
loqui equitatem.

Dilexisti omnia uerba precipita
tionis: lingua dolosa.

Propterea deus destruet te in fi
nem: euellet te ⁊ emigrabit te de
tabernaculo tuo ⁊ radicem tuam

missing from the Macclesfield Psalter. The close
correspondence between its surviving images and
those in the related manuscripts mentioned above
suggests, however, that the story of Jonah and the
whale may have been depicted at Psalm 68 and that of
Jacob's dream at Psalm 80, while the personification
of the Church probably introduced Psalm 101. This
eclectic approach, historical, liturgical and
interpretative, is strikingly different from the
uniformly straightforward illustration of the biblical
text favoured in the majority of fourteenth-century
Psalters. It revives the iconographic programme
established in English Psalters in the early thirteenth-
century and raises intriguing questions about the

mino canticum nouum: quia mi
rabilia fecit.

aluauit sibi dextra eius: et bra
chium sanctum eius.

otum fecit dominus salutare suu:
in conspectu gencium reuelauit i
uiciam suam.

Recordatus est misedie sue: et

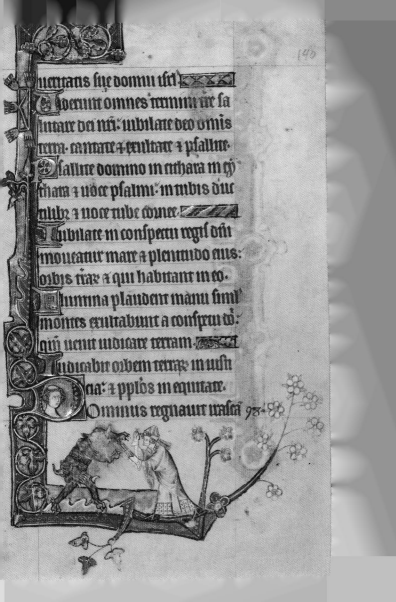

uertatis fue domni istl

hiderunt omnes termini tre sa
lutare dei nri: iubilate deo o mis
terra· cantate 7 eultate 7 psallite·

Psallite domino in cithara in cy
thara 7 uoce psalmi· in tubis du
ctilib3 7 uoce tube cornee·

Iubilate in conspectu regis dni·
moueatur mare 7 plenitudo eius:
orbis trax 7 qui habitant in eo·

Flumina plaudent manu simul
montes exultabunt a conspectu dni:
qui uenit iudicare terram·

Iudicabit orbem terraru in iusti
cia: 7 pplos in equitate·

Ominus regnauit irascal

RIGHT:
Isiah praying
(fol. 207v,
detail)

OVERLEAF:
Death strikes
(fols. 235v-
236r, detail)

archaising tastes of the East Anglian artists and their patrons a century later.

Historiated initials introduce the other two major text divisions in the Macclesfield Psalter. The prophet Isaiah prays to the Lord at the beginning of the Canticles. Particularly arresting are the images opening the Office of the Dead, the text read before a funeral and as a regular prayer for the dead, as well as a constant reminder of mortal human nature. A young man is admonished of his ultimate fate – the final stroke of Death, his wife's grief, and his only hope, a salvation from God above – while the activities performed in the margins below are less solemn.

laudate eum in tympano ↄ
choro: laudate eũ in cordis ↄ orga
laudate eum in cymba C̄uo.
sus beneconantibꝯ: laudate eum ĩ
cymbalis iubilacõis omnis sp̃s
lauter dñm.
Onfitebor t
domineqⁿ
ꝓratus es m̃.
conũsus est
furor tuus
ↄ consolatus es me.
cce deus saluator meus: fidu
cialiter agam ↄ non timebo.
Quia fortitudo mea ↄ laus mea
dñs: ↄ fc̄s est michi in salutem.

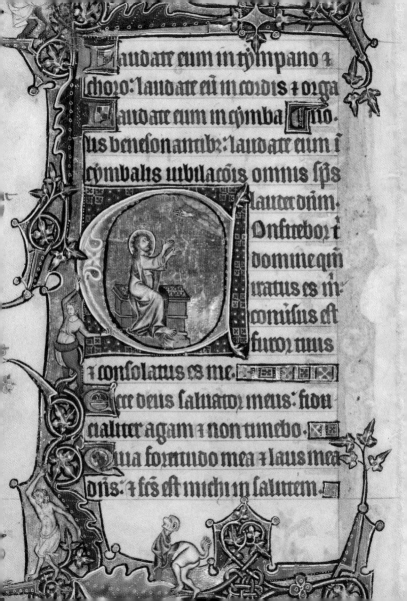

mino in regione uiuor. ps. Dilexi qm.

x. Heu me quia incolatus meus plo

gatus est. ps. Ad dnm cum trib. x. Dns

custodit te ab omni malo custodiat a

nimam tuam dns. ps. Leuaui. x. Si

iniquitates obseruaueris dne dne qs

sustinebit. ps. De profundis. a. Opa

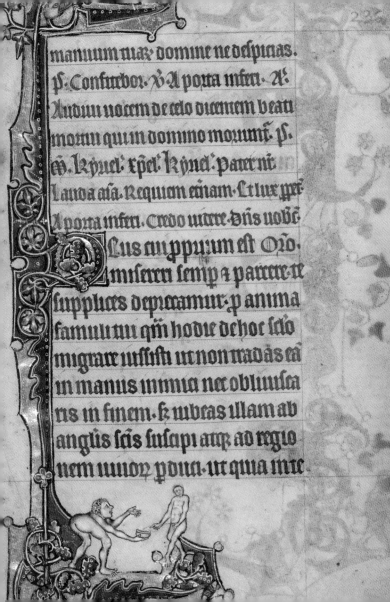

manuum tuar: domine ne despicias.

ps. Confitebor. V̄ A porta inferi. R̄:

Audiui uocem de celo dicentem beati

mortui qui in domino moriuntur. ps.

em. Kyriel' xpel' kyriel' pater nr

lauda aia. Requiem eternam. Et lux ppe

A porta inferi. Credo uidere Dns uobc

Deus cui pprium est Oro.

miserere semp & parcere te

supplices deprecamur: p anima

famuli tui qm hodie de hoc seo

migrare iussisti ut non tradas ea

in manus inimica nec obliuisca

ris in finem. & iubeas illam ab

angelis scis suscipi atqz ad regio

nem inuior pduci: ut quia in te

The marginalia

The marginal humour and uninhibited fantasy are the most charming and provocative aspects of the Macclesfield Psalter. Hybrid creatures merge human and animal shapes into nightmarish visions. A fox grabs a credulous cockerell or runs away with the farmer's wife's duck. An ape-doctor tricks a bear-patient with a mock diagnosis. An enormous skate fish frightens a man out of his wits. Wielding a sword against a giant snail seems pointless. Rabbits joust, play organs or ride the hounds that are supposed to hunt them. A lady rejects the advances of a suitor with an eloquently projecting sword, or is poised in a choice between the courtly love of a gallant horseman and the beastly lust of a wildman. The bawdy verges on the scatological, with animals and humans exposing their posteriors or peering into each other's bottoms.

The sources of these pictorial parodies, absurdities and obscenities were both verbal and

RIGHT:
The ape-doctor and his bear-patient (fol. 22r, detail)

32

qui ingreditur sine macula · A
operatur iusticiam · ▦▦▦▦
Qui loquitur ueritatem in cord
suo: qui non egit dolis in ling si
ec fecit primo suo malum ·
obpbrium non accepit aduisu
 proximos suos ·

quam retribuisti nobis

Beatus qui tenebit et allidet: pa
uulos suos ad petram.

Confitebor tibi domine in toto
corde meo: quoniam audisti uerba

oris mei.

LEFT:
The stag
(fol. 193v,
detail)

RIGHT:
The giant
skate (fol.
68r, detail)

OVERLEAF:
A bishop's
blessing and
its parody
(fols. 169v–
170r, detail)

visual. They range from the *exempla*, or anecdotes used by preachers to spice up their sermons, to religious plays, secular romances, and *fabliaux* that entertained courtly audiences and townsfolk alike. Visual parallels abound in the 'margins' of medieval churches and cathedrals, the stone gargoyles on their facades, and the misericords, the carved wooden seats of the stalls inside the choir. The latter visualize not only literary examples, but also social realities, such as the punishment of adultery with riding a horse backwards that features in the Macclesfield Psalter as well. By far the most numerous sources were illuminated manuscripts. Bestiaries offered a menagerie of real and mythical animals, all equipped with a moralizing Christian message. Hybrid creatures with swan-like necks

domine labium me tac o dne

ueneps pare: benedictus qui uenit

in nomine domini.

Benedicimus uobis de domo do

mini: deus dns + illuxit nobis.

onstitui te diem sollempnem

in condensis: usq; ad cornu altaris.

eus meus es tu + 9fitebor tibi

deus meus es tu + exaltabo te.

onfitebor tibi qm exaudisti me:

+ fcs es michi in salutem

onfitemini dno qm bonus:

quoniam in fclm mifcdia eius.

Lati immaculati in uia: q

amblant in lege domini.

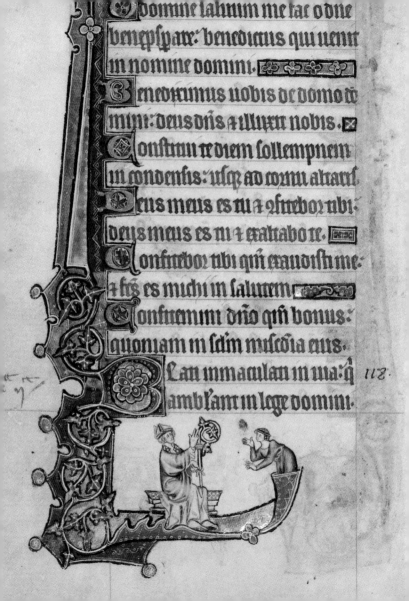

in toto corde exquirunt eum.
on enim qui operantur iniquita
tem: in uiis eius ambulauerunt.
u mandasti: mandata tua cus
todiri nimis.
tinam dirigantur uie mee: ad
custodiendas iustificacoes tuas.
unc non confundar: cum perspexero
in omnibz mandatis tuis.
onfitebor tibi in direccoe cordis:
in eo qd didici iudicia iusticie tue.
ustificacoes tuas custodiam:
non me derelinquas usqz quaqz.
n quo corrigit adolescencior ui
am suam: in custodiendo sermo

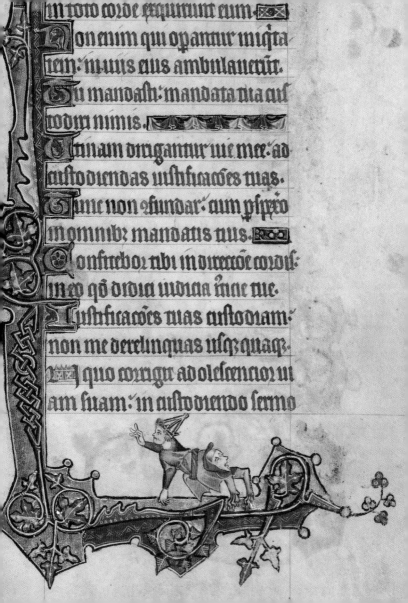

and hunched backs extended from the foliage decoration of Bolognese legal manuscripts that were reaching English ecclesiastical and University centers by the early fourteenth century.

Identifying the sources of these images does not, however, explain their meaning in the margins of an individual manuscript. Pattern sheets and model books, such as the famous one in Cambridge (Magdalene College, Pepys MS 1916), included many of them as stock motifs, ready for recycling. The artists of the East Anglian manuscripts combined and re-used them in a variety of contexts. Numerous marginal figures in the Gorleston Psalter are reminiscent of cardboard puppets. The gold fields between their limbs are probably leftovers from the

RIGHT:
Exposure
(fol. 138v,
detail)

ABOVE:
An ape
peering in a
man's
bottom
(fol. 45v,
detail)

background that supported them in the exemplar, before the artist decided to re-use them as freestanding figures. They have almost disappeared in the Macclesfield Psalter, but it preserves another clue for the transfer and re-use of designs. The pricks around the image of the stag, one of the most favourite subjects in contemporary manuscript borders, are evidence of the pouncing technique, although we cannot be certain of its date. The Macclesfield marginalia draw on numerous motifs found in the Gorleston Psalter, but supplement them with many new themes, and transform the large, bold shapes to miniature visions of exquisite finesse. This expanded and refined repertoire then enters the Douai Psalter, but concentrates only at its major text divisions, on some ten pages or so. The rest, though elegant, are fairly plain and restrained, quite unlike the pages of the Macclesfield Psalter, peppered with satire and scandal throughout.

What was the role of, and the justification for, such images in the Book of Psalms – the text central to medieval liturgy and devotion? No doubt, they beautified the book and amused its reader. But their function was hardly limited to the effect of slapstick humour. Nor was it 'marginal', despite their position on the page. Laughter was not forbidden in the Middle Ages. It was part of every-day life, even at the heart of religious experience, as the exempla, misericords, and plays reveal. This holistic and healthy attitude to life, accommodating the saints

RIGHT:
A classical nude pointing at the text (fol. 110v, detail)

tanquam f

Et appoſi

and the sinners, and embracing the world in all its shapes and colours, springs from the pages of the Macclesfield Psalter without prejudice or false modesty. The rigid distinction between sacred and profane, high and low, serious and funny, was more foreign to medieval than to post-medieval mentality. The marginal obscenities, perfectly acceptable to the medieval patron of the Macclesfield Psalter, clearly offended the puritanical sentiments of its post-medieval owners. They defaced both horned devils and bare bottoms, equating evil with laughter. In the Middle Ages,

laughter could wage war on evil. It could warn against sin through negative example, as its disturbingly realistic depiction implicated the viewer. It could reinforce moral values and social order by exposing and lampooning their violation. It could defeat boredom, distraction and sloth by keeping one alert through the long hours of public prayer or private reading. Indeed, many seemingly random grotesques in the margins of the Macclesfield Psalter draw the reader's attention to the text of the Psalms by providing a subtle visual pun or pointing emphatically at a phrase or even a

RIGHT:
Grotesque
(fol. 41v,
detail)

syllable. Such 'word-images' encouraged a close examination of the text, teased the reader-viewer, stimulated associative thinking, provided visual anchors for the memory, opened short-cuts in finding one's way around the book, and offered incentives for repeated and continuous reading. The marginalia were – and still are – central to the experience of the Macclesfield Psalter.

piens in corde suo·non est deus·

orrupti sunt 4 abhominabi

les fci sunt in iniquitatib; non

est qui faciat bonum·

eus de celo pspexit super filios

hominum: ut uideat si est intelli

gens aut requirens deum·

mnes declinauerunt simul i

The artist

The strongest evidence about the importance of the marginal imagery in the Macclsfield Psalter is their artistic execution. They share the precious pigments, advanced techniques, and exquisite refinement of the miniatures and historiated initials, adding significantly to the cost of the book and therefore approved by the patron. The artist lavished as much attention on the facial expressions, sophisticated coiffures, and delicately modelled fabrics of marginal figures as he did on the central protagonists. The opening pages of Psalms 52 and 97 demonstrate his playful attitude to the size, scale and level of detail in the initials and borders. Both main and marginal figures demonstrate his

LEFT:
David and
the fool;
portrait
busts and
ploughing
scene
(fol. 77r,
detail)

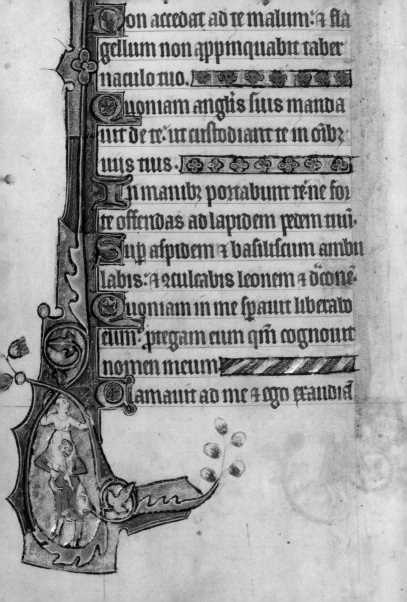

on accedat ad te malum: ⁊ fla-
gellum non appꝛopinquabit tabernaculo tuo.

Quoniam anglis suis manda-
uit de te: ut custodiant te in oibʒ
uijs tuis.

In manibʒ poꝛtabunt te ne foꝛ-
te offendas ad lapidem pedem tuũ.

Sup aspidem ⁊ basiliscum ambu-
labis: ⁊ ꝯculcabis leonem ⁊ dꝛconē.

Quoniam in me spauit liberabo
eum: pꝛtegam eum qm̅ cognouit
nomen meum.

lamauit ad me ⁊ ego exaudia

ongitudine dieꝛ replebo eum:
⁊ ostendam illi salutare meum.

Bonum est confiteri dño:
psallere noī tuo altissime.

Ad annunciandum mane mise
ricordiam tuam: ⁊ ueritatem tuā
p noctem.

In decacoꝛdo psalterio: cum cā
tico in cythara.

Quia delectasti me dñe in factura
tua: ⁊ in opibꝛ manuū tuaꝛ exulta

Quam magnificata sunt opa tua domine: nimis pfunte
ſtē sunt cogitaciones tue.

exceptional modelling of subtle violets and greens, and his innovative use of an unusual glittering pigment. This may well be one of the earliest examples of mosaic gold in East Anglian manuscripts; it appears in small, experimental areas of the Stowe Breviary, but is entirely missing from the Gorleston Psalter. The artist of the Macclesfield Psalter has mastered it to the full, creating tangible effects of volume and texture.

The illusion of depth is enhanced by another playful use of the marginalia. Figures emerge from the dense foliage to support the Psalm initials, draw the reader's attention to a particular passage, and engage in activities that continue across the page or extend beyond the physical confines of the book and into the viewer's reality. The rendering of the human body in a classical fashion and with the utmost anatomical precision place the Macclesfield Psalter among the early examples of the 'Italianate' trend in fourteenth-century English painting. Its most striking aspect is the unprecedented interest in the inner life of the individual. The attempt to capture fleeting human emotions and the

PREVIOUS PAGE: Acrobats, an archer, and St John the Baptist (fols. 132v-133r, detail)

RIGHT:
The 'athlete'
(fol. 28v,
detail)

virtuoso depiction of their extremes are the salient features of the Macclesfield Master. His sorrowful, anguished portraits are deeply moving, strikingly modern and sophisticated, truly unforgettable.

Yet, the gracefully swaying figures with dainty features and the three-headed monsters with hairy noses are equally characteristic of this versatile artist. His repertoire is so vast and his juxtapositions of large and small, serious and ludicrous are so striking as to suggest the involvement of more than one illuminator in the Macclesfield Psalter. Indeed, at least two assistants decorated the borders and may have painted designs sketched by the Master.

The division of labour requires much further research, but similar patterns of very close collaboration are found in the Stowe Breviary and the Douai Psalter. Christopher de Hamel identified the Macclesfield Master with one of the two main illuminators of the Douai Psalter, the so-called Douai Psalter Assistant.

Another manuscript preserving painting by the Macclesfield Master is crucial for our understanding of his working environment. A copy of Bede's *Ecclesiastical History* in Cambridge (Trinity College, MS R.7.3) shows the Macclesfield Master collaborating with the Douai Master. Marginal themes from the Macclesfield Psalter reappear in the borders of the Trinity Bede. This modest book preserves a curious feature not found in the contemporary Psalters. Five of its six illuminated leaves were marked with inscriptions, e.g. 'the tenth leaf of the third gathering', to ensure their return to the right place in the volume after they were illuminated. This suggests two distinct locations for the copying of the text and the painting of the six leaves. Unlike the East Anglian Psalters, the Trinity Bede was copied by at least four hands. They followed the example set in the first few lines of the prologue and Book V by an expert scribe. With its peculiar methods of production and as yet unidentified arms on the fore-edge, the Trinity Bede raises intriguing questions about the context in which the Macclesfield and Douai Masters worked.

RIGHT:
Bird man
(fol. 40v,
detail)

in hos p dnm nrm ihm xpm.
repcbiscant in pace· Amen·
non uineiam armu je.....

in carcere p Onfiteor tibi dne
nudos· non pater celi ⁊ terre iqz
non potan benignissime ac to
pntatibz: sed ne ihu cum sco spu
coram scis anglis tuis ⁊ coram p
senti altari mo· quia in pctis nat
sum· ⁊ in pctis nutritus ⁊ peccis
post baptisma usqz ad hanc horā
sum uersatus· confiteor ⁊ quia
pecaui nimis in supbia tam ui
sibili qm inuisibili· in nana gla

The patron

Who was the patron that could afford such a lavishly illuminated book and appreciate both its sophisticated refinement and bold humour? The remaining East Anglian Psalters are imposing volumes, presentation copies, symbols of wealth and status. The Macclesfield Psalter, though more than a match for their richness and beauty, is half their size. It was not a coffee-table book. It was intended for private prayer, for the most intimate use of an individual. Its original owner remains

LEFT:
Man praying
at an altar (fol.
250r, detail)

elusive, but a tempting suggestion has been made. The candidate is John, the eighth Earl of Warenne (1286–1347). He is the likeliest patron of the Gorleston Psalter, which displays his arms prominently and has its borders populated by rabbits in their warrens, a visual pun on the owner's name. Rabbits are the commonest creatures in Gothic margins, second only to monkeys, but in the Gorleston Psalter they are far more numerous than in any contemporary book. The only manuscripts in which they appear in comparable numbers are those made for the family of Joan de Bar who married the Earl of Warenne in 1306. The Fitzwilliam Museum preserves one of them, the Metz Pontifical which was made for Renaut de Bar, Bishop of Metz (1303–1316). The Macclesfield

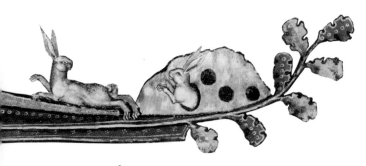

Psalter features rabbits on no more than five pages. The scenes follow the compositions of the Gorleston Psalter so faithfully as to suggest the re-use of themes that have entered the artists' repertoire as stock motifs. This is confirmed by the similar recycling of the ploughing scene, David and Goliath, the cat and the mouse, the snail combat, and the stag hunt – all motifs that feature in the Gorlseton Psalter and reappear with little or no alteration in the Macclesfield Psalter and

...inis pulgr...illam... hec in m...

t legem tuam non sum oblitus.

Media nocte surgebam ad ofiten=
dum tibi: sup iudicia inficacois

Particeps ego sum oīm
timentium te: a custodientiū mā=
data tua.

Mīa tua dñe plena est terra: iusti=
ficacoēs tuas doce me.

Bonitatem fecisti cum seruo
tuo domine: secūdm verbum tuū

Bonitatem a disciplinā tuū.
a sciencia doce me: quia in man

two of the other manuscripts illuminated by its
artist, the Douai Psalter and the Trinity Bede.

Similarly inconclusive is the heraldic evidence
of the Macclesfield Psalter. Unlike the Gorleston
Psalter which displays numerous shields, an
impressive roll-call of the most powerful English
aristocratic families, the Macclesfield Psalter
preserves a single coat of arms identified by Anne
Payne as that of the Gorges family. It appears only
twice, in a line ending on fol. 19v and in the border
of fol. 37v. Its position is not prominent enough to
suggest direct patronage, but it deserves further
consideration, since it recurs more than once in a
manuscript closely related to the Macclesfield
Psalter, the Stowe Breviary.

Stronger evidence may have been lost with
several of the missing or mutilated leaves, notably
the excised initial and border of the Confession
prayer. The *bas-de-page* shows a young
layman praying at an altar. The same
person is probably depicted praying in
bed at Psalm 114. The unusually

nia·a utga ao mues uemas nia·

ABOVE:
A Dominican
friar (fol. 158v,
detail)

detailed text of the Confession prayer mentions the
handling of the sacred vessels and the body of
Christ with unclean hands and heart, indifference
to the poor, and neglect of the services in church.
The wording may suggest a clerical, monastic or
mendicant patron. Curiously, a Dominican friar is
shown in prayer beneath Psalm 107. However, he is
not a likely owner of a manuscript whose Calendar
and Litany exclude St Dominic. On the other hand,
the wording of the Confession prayer may not refer
to administering the Eucharist, celebrating the
divine office or performing pastoral duties, but
rather to taking Communion without confession,
lack of concentration in church, and neglect of alms

giving, all failures for which a good Christian would have to repent. A Dominican confessor would have been quick to point that out and may have even suggested the wording of the prayer. Its numerous references to temptations and sins of the flesh mirror the marginal imagery of the Macclesfield Psalter. If its owner had any doubts about their message, the Confession prayer would have made it clear. This is not to say that he was denied the pleasure and amusement we find in them today. The Macclesfield Psalter will have many more delights to offer as research on it has only just begun. Such a fascinating discovery will challenge and reward generations of students. Its new home will welcome thousands of visitors to marvel at its beauty. This book is an invitation to all who wish to study and enjoy it.

Stella Panayotova
Keeper of Manuscripts and Printed Books
The Fitzwilliam Museum

m fortitudo mea et
refugium meum es tu: et propter no
men tuum deduces me et enutries me.
Educes me de laqueo quem abscon
derunt michi: quoniam tu es pro
tector meus.
In manus tuas commendo spiritum
meum: redemisti me domine de
us veritatis.
Odisti observantes vanitatem.

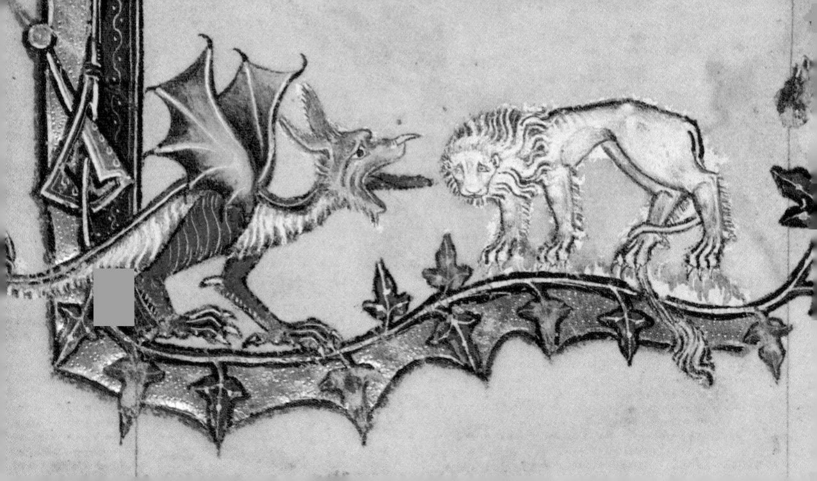

The Macclesfield Psalter (MS 1-2005) was purchased by The Fitzwilliam Museum, University of Cambridge, with grants from the National Heritage Memorial Fund, the National Art Collections Fund, the Friends of the Fitzwilliam Museum, the Friends of the National Libraries, the Cadbury Trust, and with contributions from a public appeal launched by the National Art Collections Fund.

Further reading

S.C. Cockerell, *The Gorleston Psalter*, London, 1907

L.F. Sandler, *Gothic Manuscripts 1285–1385*, A Survey of Manuscripts Illuminated in the British Isles, vol. 5, Oxford, 1986

C.S. Hull, 'The Douai Psalter and Related East Anglian Manuscripts', Ph.D. thesis, Yale University, 1994

M. McIlwain, 'The Gorleston Psalter: A Study of the Marginal in the Visual Culture of Fourteenth-Century England', Ph.D. thesis, Institute of Fine Arts, New York, 1999

The Library of the Earls of Macclesfield removed from Shirburn Castle, Part Three: Western Manuscripts, Sotheby's, London, 22 June 2004

F. Law-Turner, *The Ormesby Psalter*, Oxford, 2005

LEFT:
A dragon and a lion (fol. 43v, detail)

First published in 2005 by
The Fitzwilliam Museum
Trumpington Street | Cambridge CB2 1RB
Tel : 01223 332900 | Fax : 01223 332923
Email: fitzmuseum-enquiries@lists.cam.ac.uk

www.fitzmuseum.cam.ac.uk

RIGHT:
Grotesques
(fol. 11r, detail)

ISBN: 0-904454-70-3

FRONT COVER:
The
Annunciation
to the
Shepherds
(fol. 139v,
detail)

Text: Stella Panayotova
Photography: Andrew Morris
Project editors: Fiona Brown & Thibault Catrice
Design: cantellday www.cantellday.co.uk
Produced by Fitzwilliam Museum Enterprises Ltd
Printed by Graphicom srl, Vicenza, Italy

Cum inuocarem exa

me deus iusticie mee

bulacõe dilatasti michi

serere mei · 7 exaudi oroem

lli hominum usq; quo

corde · ut quid diligitis uan

7 queritis mendacium

ur pater

t super

ouiam